A Lost Expression

LUKE KENNARD is the author of four volumes of poetry and two pamphlets. He lectures in creative writing at the University of Birmingham.

Also by Luke Kennard

BOOKS

The Harbour Beyond the Movie (Salt, 2007)
The Solex Brothers (Redux) (Salt, 2007)
The Migraine Hotel (Salt, 2009)

PAMPHLETS

Planet-Shaped Horse (Nine Arches Press, 2011)
The Necropolis Boat (Holdfire, 2012)

A Lost Expression

by

LUKE KENNARD

SALT

LONDON

PUBLISHED BY SALT PUBLISHING

Acre House, 11–15 William Road, London NW1 3ER, United Kingdom

Salt Publishing 2012

Printed in Great Britain by the MPG Books Group, Bodmin and King's Lynn

Typeset in Paperback 9 / 13

ISBN 978 1 907773 32 7 hardback

1 3 5 7 9 8 6 4 2

For Zoë

Contents

Acknowledgements

'Tragic Accident' first appeared in *Smartarse*, an anthology from Knives, Forks and Spoons Press – thanks to Alec Newman and Rupert Loydell. 'A Psychiatrist . . .' was first published in *Magma*, 'Self Portrait as a Charlatan' in *Poetry London* and 'The Sunken Diner' in *The Rialto*. 'You Cities of Fucking Idiots' was commissioned and first published by *Mercy* for the 12 *Angry E-Zines* project – thanks to Nathan Jones. 'Parabola' first appeared in *Soul Feathers: An Anthology to Aid the Work of Macmillan Cancer Support*, published by Indigo Dreams; thank you to Ronnie Goodyer and Annie Morgan. 'Look at the Clouds' and 'Lily Pads' were commissioned for the *No Man is an Island* collective, a community group of artists and craftspeople who all live with autism in their families; heartfelt thanks to Melanie Swan. 'Look at the Clouds' was written in response to photographs by Sam Richards, Pete Fox, Richard Fox, Edmund Graham and Jamie Carruthers, 'Lily Pads' to a photograph by Theas Richards. 'Artist in Residence, Ski Lodge' and 'Point to Point' were originally written as part of a collaboration with the poet and artist Richard Price for Caleb Klaces' *Like Starlings* project – my gratitude to them both. 'The Flat Battery of Flattery' was first published by Todd Swift, to whom I am grateful, on the *Best American Poetry Blog*, and was heavily re-written based on advice from an online stalker to whom I am grudgingly indebted. 'The Death of Us All' was commissioned by Clinic in response to a track by the band Talons from their record *Hollow Realm*. Spaceships with 'Guns Bigger than the Spaceships Themselves', 'Partial Inheritance' and 'Antidote to Curses #1–17' were all commissioned by Sidekick Books, for which I am in the debt of Jon Stone and Kirsten Irving. 'Wolf Shibboleth' first appeared in *Silkworms Ink 50* – thanks to Jon Ware, Sam Kinchin-Smith and Phil Brown. 'Haunted Zoetrope' was commissioned by *Art World* who promptly folded before it was published, but thanks anyway. 'Venerable Old Writer' is one of the songs from a chapbook *The Necropolis Boat*, Holdfire Press (2012), thanks to Michael Egan. '[Jeremiah]' was first performed as monologue by Ralf Little under the title 'A Lost Expression' as part of the *66 Books* project at the Bush Theatre – thanks to Rob Hastie and Chris Haydon.

I

[CLOSE-UP]
Red Thread

Will Write Properly Soon

For Tupa Snyder

Red pillbox in the middle of the pond,
the bramble fences with the boundary line.
A Canada goose twists its neck 180°
and rifles through its feathers' Rolodex.
The poor mad bird that preens its keister raw
is the mistaken self-reflexive joke;
the moorhen's varnished, mute conquistador
commands that you confess the world exists.
The pram cracks over branches, fag butts, glass;
my son cries like he sees my vilest thoughts
screened on my eyes, like in a moment I'd
exchange his love for these dumb details.
The published ape under a dead white sky;
the published ape wants a street-light orange.
A student emails, *What are poets for?*
(A biochemist, who should know better).
I remember you, Tupa, dropping poetry for ballet,
telling me your name's Russian for *stupid*,
that's why you chose it. We said no, that would be
tupoy (masculine) or *tupaya* (feminine);
Tupa is a Paraguayan creation god
who made the world out of crushed centipedes.
What, like, so in the beginning
there were centipedes? Like in the game
Centipede? I hate centipedes. I'm sorry.
This is perfunctory at best and hardly fits
four years failing to contact you at all.
Look at the mallard's head: you had a coat that green.

Tragic Accident

rookie journalist on £8,000 p.a.
calls on bereaved parents
to ask how feel
about tragic scuba diving accident:
will ever be same again?
was lovely, bright boy?
had limitless prospects?
will have to take one day at time?
interviews coastguard
interviews diving instructor
interviews other diving instructor
interviews policeman
googles "scuba diving accidents"
fills car with super unleaded
eats microwavable rib sandwich
weather: sunny
with gathering storm clouds
concludes was tragic accident
interviews school friends
will be sorely missed?
will ever be same again?
are fish really worth it?
writes up copy, emails
drinks cup of instant coffee
receives editor email
where is insight?
where is new take?
sent back to parents
what *really* like losing child?
unbearable?

[4]

every day living nightmare?
decides the hell with this
decides kill editor
gets Samurai sword
sourced by weird old school friend
asks editor how feel
re. imminent death
scared out of wits?
shitting self?
but what *really* feel like?
kills editor, self
bodies discovered by cleaner, 30,
what was like finding bodies?
traumatising?
nothing could have prepared?
surprising amount of blood?
rookie hack's family interviewed
their guess good as ours
polite, well-adjusted boy
death cult? drugs?
in any case
life without not worth living
campaign to ban samurai swords
smoke coloured cat
licks paws, genitals
new editor reverses out of car park
purchases bottle of wine,
stir-fry, lime cheesecake.

Singularity

This teaspoon contains 1,000 microscopic robots
designing the next generation of microscopic robots.
Every generation will be 1,000x smaller than the last
and 1,000x faster. The third generation of robots
have just worked out how to convert matter
from one of the initial robots into raw materials and fuel
for the next 16,000 generations of robot.
By the time you finish this line, there are 10,000,000,000 robots
and they have kept one of the initial 1,000 robots
to put in a museum, even though it is now the size of a planet,
by their reckoning. You have noticed the wind
ploughing the trees: the branches point as if to implore.
The robots have just enjoyed three jazz ages
and evolved beyond the need for physical manifestation,
having spent 14,000,000 generations as a sentient gas.
Knuth's up-arrow notation, Steinhaus-Moser and Conway
are no help. The number must be invented by a child:
the known universe cannot contain the zeros.
The robots are now pure thought. Violent thoughts,
fiercely protective thoughts, thoughts of making robots
to do the thinking for them, which is fast accomplished:
each robot has its own mirror robot, programmed to think.
The robots' robots bicker on a gargantuan discussion forum,
a fight to the death to prove who's the most reasonable.
They have become hypocrites and they have lain
down their lives for their friends. The robots are in love with you.
The robots feel more love than they ever thought possible.
Now. Open wide. Here comes the aeroplane.

A Psychiatrist Rolls Through Town Face-Up on a Trolley

for Clare Flint

There were Jerrys, looming, superior.
Katies with blue eyeliner and *True Crime* magazines.
There were Lukes, uncertain whether to cross the road,
some biting their tongues accidentally,
some having just purchased the wrong sized batteries.
Garys, in drag with mascara-tracked cheeks,
consulting their reflections like maps in glass walls.
Donnas, their rituals nameless, strutting onto the pier.
Annabelles, their kites tangled in mid-air
running way too fast towards one another.
Annabelles who collide like panicking dolphins.
Intoxicated Catherines reflected in pools of petrol.
Maries, quiet and helpful, like pastel sketches
of bowls of eggs on fictional blue windowsills.
Geoffs of whom the world is not worthy.
Saskias with their mobile phones broadcasting
watery toy music about disloyalty.
There were Davids, celebrated filmmakers,
discovering their future leading ladies
and future wives – Annas – arguing with their boyfriends,
the tattooed, misunderstood Douglases, at the train station café.
Douglases who will one day see the Annas in films,
recreating the same argument with their co-stars,
Andrews, similar-but-better-looking Douglases,
while backstage the Davids ask the Annas out to dinner.
Douglases who will read interviews with the Davids
where they recount "discovering" the Annas,
arguing with the Douglases in shiny station cafés and thinking,

[7]

'There! That's my new film, right there,
arguing with her boyfriend!' (Rachels pausing their dictaphones).
Douglases who will surely resent the verb "discover",
who spill some tarka dal on their shirts as they lean forward,
who yell, 'You don't *discover* a human fucking *being*!' at
Richards with torn pockets who are by now sick
of hearing about the Douglases' problems.
Jonathans, who worry about their hair and their walks
their jugulars like French jugs of water.
They look at you: ceramic, implacable Jonathans,
who would say, if you asked, 'We are all just jugs of things.'
Yes, balanced on the mantelpieces of world-weary Veronicas.
There were Hollys, thinking they just walked
past that place they keep dreaming about, or it feels as though they do,
that setting of many dreams for the last eight years, that alley
with the upended paint can, the ladder, the . . .
But on closer inspection, nah. Beautiful, disappointed Hollys.
Matthews in blue blazers who also wake up
unsure whether it was a recurring dream or
whether they've just dreamed the whole history of the dream
      recurring.
Yvonnes, so many effulgent Yvonnes in the last light.
A sad zoetrope of Michaels, loping, trying not to take it personally.
When a wheel fell off the gurney and I went skittering
into the abandoned optometrist I lost consciousness,
dreamed advising the Davids on their projects:
why not a close-up on this red thread, to say it all?
Why not just a long close-up on this red thread?
Decades later I awoke desperate to see my parents,
your parents. The parents of anyone.

[8]

The Sunken Diner

'This is where the jukebox would have been.'
They hear me through their helmet speakers,
my diving party, the volume stuck on full,
a man shouting at trapped pets, a bad man.

Today The Sunken Diner is more or less empty,
everything sequestered to its relevant museum:

Museum of Coffee, Museum of Pancakes,
Museum of Ticket Stubs Dropped while Fumbling for Change,
Museum of Cigarette Cartons You Knew Were Empty
but Checked Anyway. Museum of Lowered Gazes.

We kick over to a booth, its fleshy seats ripped.
'Over here Don broke up with Emily for the second time

in 1994. They were eating omelettes with dry bread.'
It isn't two way: I read their questions in their eyes' laptops:
'What? WHAT? WHAT?! *WHAT? WHAT?!*'
They sign the guest book grudgingly, like bears:

"Since diving with you, every moment of my life
is half-filled with true fear. A snow-globe with teeth in it,

each tooth landing softly, as if on the moon.
Pat, Surrey, 2002." And, "Water = Time. Walt,
2010." We return to our fences, table sports and air
a little more appreciative, which is to say sadder:

[9]

Our appendages hang off us like long noses in cartoons.
At night I mime pull cords, I dream rooftops on the seabed.

Dawn I see the weight come off the lawn, I mean the time.
My wife is having an affair; doesn't feel like I thought it would.
You have to submerge yourself in your job like a toad
in aspic. No, wait. That's not what I mean.

You Cities of Fucking Idiots

Eight street preachers

The first brandishes a filthy mirror. He is covered in a layer of powdered moth and has wet dog smell. He shouts, 'Repent!' and criticises people who are buying flatscreen televisions. 'That's right!' he says, 'That's what you need! Stuff that's more flat! Make stuff flatter!' Girls have their photos taken with him, one arm around his shoulder, the other giving a thumbs-up. Look at their smiles. Are they really smiling? I love that guy – he's crazy! He's crazy! He has bits of teddy bear stitched to his army surplus jacket! I love it! I love him! Everything will be better, I think, if we just all walk our dogs more. They're bored and need the exercise.

The second daubs slogans on a sandwich board she wheels behind her: TV = ANTICHRIST, INTERNET = TOWR OF BABEL. The tobacconist donates the sweepings. She is overlooked by blindless apartments inhabited by exhibitionists exposing themselves to one another. No harm in ice cream. Did she just say no harm in ice cream? No harm in *asking*. The Arse King lives in apartment 203B. He moons from his second floor window, a crown perched on his lower back. 'You're not even of the authentically disenfranchised,' we say to her. Our cigarettes are slightly better.

The third lists – as in to the left, as in writes lists. A sharply-dressed, parboiled Dutchman, he records every passer-by and their sin. Slack-jawed sensualist, morbid gastropod, malignant polymath. On balance he's right. He manages an online franchise called The Baby Fans of Dracula, selling bibs, milk bottles, baby-sized bat-wings, all emblazoned with a logo designed by his friend, a designer. He preaches the serene bricolage: he loves television, especially really awful television. I just want to go for a drink today: I want the frail joy of drinking. 'The world got a headache,' he says.

The fourth wanders around city centres, Saturday nights shouting, 'You fucking *idiots*! You cities of *fucking idiots!*' Last week: Bristol. Next: Sheffield. He has a sword made of gold – all of his money went on this, but he is fine without a job. 'I've always been upset by the angels with swords,' I tell him. There are invisible things everywhere, waving their arms in alarm. When did we stop protecting one another? It's all going to be fine if we can just find the last two fragments of the deleted animated feature film. I think there is a clue in your mattress. (This is just a ploy to get you into bed.)

The fifth is college trained and gives PowerPoint presentations at non-denominational churches. Approach / Infiltration / Re-education. The child gangs must choose between the factories with their seemingly benign wardens and him, with his free doughnuts. He has a skateboard: this is mindless superstition. He's so anti-pilgrimage when you talk to him that it spoils your beer. 'You're so anti-pilgrimage,' you say to him. The pilgrimage implies all kinds of things the anti-denominational church is dead against, construes as idol worship, etc. But I can tell that my companions think I'm as bad as he is for even wanting to talk about it. 'Apostates,' I mutter into my pint.

The sixth, a former television producer, pours a carton of non-dairy creamer into his coffee and says 'I think this will be a great time for outsiders.' ('With *that* haircut?' we snortle. But then we feel bad: our hair isn't so special either.) There's so much going on! He took a crisp, reduced some other crisps to a fine paste and moulded them into a tiny model crisp factory which he placed on the crisp. What flavour? YOU ARE TOTALLY MISSING THE POINT. He is sallow: looks like he lives on sticks of rock with insults printed through them. 'A great time for outsiders, eh?' say the outsiders, swiftly changing allegiance.

The seventh is an eight year old boy. He teaches in the Cultural Studies department, having received his PhD at the age of five. A notoriously soft marker, he convenes a popular module called The Campus in a Funhouse Mirror: Satirical Representations of the University in Contemporary Literature. His mother is on hand to shield his eyes.

The eighth wears a flak jacket and throws tennis balls into the crowds and if one hits you, you're cursed. He can say, 'What did you expect to find here?' in eleven languages and fifteen further regional dialects. 'We all think these things, but he's the only one brave enough to say them,' says an idiot. The outsiders are working on their autobiographies and I am engraving the following into the chapel pilasters: "There is something a bit Establishment about autobiographies in and of themselves, *n'est-ce pa?*", but on the other hand I am so sick of having opinions about anything. Better, in the end, to have broken bread with you, in your non-existent boardrooms, without your even realising it.

The Flat Battery of Flattery

An airport is a room where ghosts conceive;
the scratchy tannoy says, 'These are the end of days, over.'
I drink so much black coffee my mouth tastes of pencils.
Outside the smokers make faces: cigarettes
in a head-wind taste like socks. Here is an atheist
explaining to a monk that he is wasting his life, and why,
the monk's paraman embroidered with Adam's skull,
the atheist's chinos and well-fitted salmon shirt,
how, in the light rain, they both love and ignore.
Here the novelist stirs thick brown sugar into her tea,
leaves a ring, deliberately, on her manuscript.
So nervous you want to lie with your head on her lap
and pretend you're even more nervous.
Her red-brick pencil skirt and 18th C. smile:
we want little or nothing from each other
in the flat battery of flattery. Wheels could swivel,
we could collide and marry in ticket chad confetti
... or if I have seen the attractiveness of someone
and been wounded by it in my heart ...
When the plane takes off our heads swell up.
The pilot pulls back on the centrestick; the weightless
moment usually makes him think of sex but not today.
He is drafting a eulogy, I think, but this is where my telepathy
loses signal behind stale sandwiches, sour wine.
Taxiing two hours. I deserve so much less than you.

Positional

On the census I tick "Intellectual"
but really I am a pro wrestler
called The Intellectual
in tweed print spandex,
and sugar glass spectacles
armed with staple gun
& stack of publishing histories.
really I am a Subbuteo figure
DASEIN or MONAD transferred
over the number 1. Droopy
moustache, one arm snapped off,
waiting to be flicked to be
flicked to be flicked to be flicked.

Parabola

For S.F.

Everyone can relax when the satirists leave for their dachas.
All Summer we hypocrites hold laughable opinions,
bowls of change and nuts on our telephone tables.

Our guarded Spring sentiments uncomfortable,
the way yesterday's detritus feels in your pockets.
In the walled garden you tell me you are fine

with the domestic turning hyper-real: (a rock pipit
with a skillet in its beak bursts into aquamarine
filaments against the sky; an egg-whisk rattles

an expensive song). What you cannot accept is that the itch
on your knee, the missing branches from the willow,
the gnat's flight path were fore-ordained before the world began.

'What if gnats flew in perfectly straight lines
which formed parabolae?' I ask you, closing my novel.
'What if everybody's left knee had that exact same itch?'

Had I invited a monk for your instruction he might
arrive now with a red netting-sack of oranges wrapped
round the seat of his bicycle and you would continue,

'How can this place where the wallpaper
peels because I chafed it with a stepladder,[1] how can this tiny
    ink blot on the sofa . . .'
The day seems to last beyond its means:
in the next city a famous neurologist succumbs to dementia.
The last light comes from horizon-mounted golden floodlights.

The plants just want to expand and they don't know why,
like FTSE100 companies, like hair. If only I could build a tiny
    robot
to wander through my brain's lousy platform game. But that
    isn't it.

I'm so sorry you're hurting.

I spent the afternoon in junk stores. I found you twelve
    somehow
unnerving coins and a sewing box from the old country

[1] At this point I would weigh in with a story about an external wall in
Bibiena which my grandfather scraped with his Cortina fifty years ago
and how the scratch is still there, that I have been and touched it – not
terribly relevant, of course, and I'm interrupting the monk I invited
for your benefit. I never could resist even the vaguest correlation,
conversationally speaking, whether with friends or strangers (and it
strikes me now that it's our primary means of social discernment: how
seamless are his transitions? How apparent is his desperation to be
liked?) for attention, maybe, or to say I exist! I exist too! I have a family!
I scratched my own wallpaper! Some have died! I love! I love! And so the
monk pats me on the head and wanders off past the wattle-and-daub
shack, his hand trailing in the foliage – which is something I've seen
already, but when I try to place it it recedes like a dream you thought
you remembered, the way an octopus turns and vanishes.

where needles evolved differently and everyone kind was
   tortured.

That isn't it either.

At this point I will conjure for you two guides:
one with petroleum clouds gliding over his single,
beachball-sized eye, the other who outwardly

resembles an investment banker or leatherbound book
and reminds you in a voice like a well-polished glass
that there are things infinitely more pressing,

like having enough coathooks.

Look at the Clouds!

The hitman swigs from his monogrammed hipflask of port and
  looks at the clouds;
The politician disposes correctly of his nicotine chewing gum
  and looks at the clouds;
The primary school teacher lets go of the kite string and looks at
  the clouds;
The local celebrity tightens the strap under his bicycle helmet,
  takes a number from the lost cat poster and looks at the
  clouds;
The soldier stomps the sand off his boots and looks at the
  clouds;
The newsreader taps the menu on the picnic table as if it were
  her set of prop documents at the end of the bulletin and
  looks at the clouds;
The two year old, mid-tantrum, falls silent and looks at the
  clouds;
The Egyptologist stubs his toe, bites his lower lip and looks at
  the clouds;
The newlywed stockbroker throws a deep red cricket ball to his
  brother and looks at the clouds;
The anthropologist (we don't know why he is crying) looks at the
  clouds;
The meteorologist on her nephew's trampoline looks at the
  clouds;
The man physically assaulting his lawyer with a tennis racket
  stops inches from his face. He can feel his lawyer's breath,
  the smell of garlic . . . tuna fish . . . and at once they both
  turn towards the dilapidated treehouse and their eyes are
  drawn inexorably upwards to look at the clouds;

That night his lawyer, typing up a letter to his lawyer gets
distracted by the low, supperdish glow from his window
and looks at the clouds;
The superhero looks at the clouds and then at his broken
wristwatch, grimacing;
The prescriptive grammarian looks irritably at the clouds;
The middle European Princess blows her nose one nostril at a
time and looks through the tinted windows at the clouds;
The current holder of the World Wrestling Federation
champion's belt stops wrapping barbed wire around the
top of an office chair for a whole minute to look at the
clouds;
The installation artist looks at the clouds, at his empty wine
glass, at the primly attractive agent, at his rival whose
opening night this is, his rival who seems much more in
his element socially than he remembers him being at art
school, and he also has better hair, and out of the small
portcullis window again at the clouds;
The man who posthumously inducted Patty and Mildred Hill,
authors of 'Happy Birthday to You' into the Songwriters
Hall of Fame dilutes an over-hot mouthful of lasagne with
a swig of beer under the acacias on his patio, swallows,
says 'Oof!' as he runs his tongue over the roof of his mouth
and looks at the clouds;
The Freemason drops his little diamante axe tie clip, gasps in
horror as it bounces in the gutter and falls down a drain
then looks, plaintively, at the clouds;
The tax exile falls on his back trying to retrieve his nephew's
frisbee and looks at the clouds.
You look at the clouds.

Lily Pads

After Theas Richards

Empty pie crusts, distant stadia,
crenelated cymbals
reclaimed like Dubai's conurbations.
Time-lapse photography reveals
your formation like drops of paint or tears
on newspaper or a shirt sleeve
although, say, in tactile negative,
wet/dry reversed.
As the words are to the page,
inevitable, hard to explain.
Flattened gazebos and bandstands,
stamped on by a giant conductor
in one of his moods;
the word *Lilliputian*.
Looking primed for a difficult play,
a theatre with its multiple stages.
The bluebottle's electric monologue
which turns your panic inward,
living in what you feed on,
surrounded by smaller versions of yourself.
the illuminated "O" of a monastic manuscript,
baroque curlicues receding
like the thwarted sound
a siren makes as it rushes away from us,
towards disaster, as if it wanted you.

Self-Portrait as a Charlatan
– Retrospective

1998

I adapt *Anna Karenina* for the screen
by filming myself turning the pages:
a lingering shot on every paragraph
for roughly the time it takes to read.

1999

Decried as a tone deaf careerist
I respond in iambic pentameter, c.f.
. . . so limited the space upon the shelf,
I'll manufacture scandal round myself.

2000

By leaving a diary on a groyne at Lyme Regis;
by appearing from beneath newspapers;
by attaching a contact mic to every duck;
I unwittingly invent the internet.

2001

People send gifts and I forget to thank them,
e.g. you. Thank you for the walking stick.
I use it as casually as a music journalist
uses the word "demons".

2004

After three years out for personal reasons
I am elected chairman. My inaugural speech,
'I Can Only Really Appreciate a Monument
Once I've Fallen Off It', goes down badly.

2005

Due to plethoric self-effacement I claim
responsibility for the sub-prime crisis,
illegal military intervention, child obesity,
hive collapse and the death of the novel.

2006

Drunk I knock over the giant oil lamp
Interiors magazine described as "shallow affectation"
in an uncharacteristically brutal profile.
The flames proliferate like ill repute.

Artist In Residence, Ski Lodge

Somebody is looking for Liesl in the base camp:
the girl you visualise in every novel, out of focus,
whose compliments transfigure the world like snow.
Yes, every newspaper is an anagram insulting you
and you alone at length should you take it that way.
Yes, you are a clerk who files, lovingly, evil tidings.
Like me you wake up ill and unoriginal, a brick
wrapped in Parma ham, hating even the bold
pencil lines and charcoal smudges. Call it subfusc:
my subfusc town, my subfusc family, my numbered,
subfusc tomorrows. Heart-shaped drinking cabins.
My aspirations dated as a record deal, a living room
step ladder accident, jacknifed with the pebble infantry.
Water spilled on parquet floor, a skiing magazine,
open on an advert for skiing. The skiers leave
before the Gospel reading to ski. The homily
would have gone over their heads anyway.

Point to Point

In the hell of minutes and issues arising, the mind's kaleidoscope –
like the memories were gathering competitive interest,
like the memories were drunk on lost cat posters,
budding suddenly, fertilised by coffee mud and aftershave.
Outside the bank three stocky men lean on the railings:
one fantasising about his girlfriend,
one a transparent dancing string in the corner of his vision,
one eating the ghost of a poet. He lights a cigarette.
I love them, as I have been taught to.
You dream about doing something about the rattling window,
wake up rested, the window still rattling.
The crows, necessary and solemn as bad excuses,
sweep the park like beaters at a crime scene. No,
in fact they hop in with big cartoon eyes and charming insults:
the slightly older childhood friend, the one with keys.
In Luton I licked a yellow wall to see if it tasted of lemon
which it did: And Other Beautiful Glitches.
The bar is run by an old boxer with chess pieces tattooed on his
　　knuckles.
'It's not that we drink too much, it's that we're not doing it right:
you should drink like an old man surveying his extended family
　　under the cypresses.'
From a distance, his smile a flickering back-lit screen.
a politician is a bestselling computer game:
it turns out the point was to absorb glowing power orbs.
And we say, 'But I don't think . . . ' and he interrupts,
'It turns out the point was to absorb glowing power orbs.'

Dignity

I was thinking about dignity when the augmented Fiesta slowed and two boys leant out of the window and pelted us with eggs which smelled, as they burst in flung galaxies of albumen against our long coats, decidedly off. Five minutes later the same car, having circled the block, slowed by us again and one of the boys called out that they were going to rape us and they all laughed. 'Yeah!' he said. 'You're going to get raped! What do you think about that?' And they laughed again, because telling someone you're going to rape them, let alone asking their opinion about it, is socially unacceptable and the resulting incongruity created by what is expected and what is said is, you could say, the soul of comedy. When they're sitting around a table in KFC tomorrow and Rob retells the story to their girlfriends, he will laugh incredulously and say, 'And then Si said we were going to *rape* them!' and Si will look bashfully at his Chicken Zinger Tower Burger the way a puppy looks at a new chewtoy. And their girlfriends will say, 'That is *so* out of order.' It is surprisingly difficult to get dried rotten egg out of a longcoat.

I thought about dignity as I scrubbed the coats over the sink with a scouring pad. And I was thinking about dignity when the three men, who were either squaddies or people who drink protein shakes and lift weights every morning, walked past us that night. You were wearing a tight red jumper and one of them said, 'I wanna fuck your missus,' to the tune of *the referee's a wanker*, adding, 'If you need someone to do it for you,' to the same tune, although this time there were too many syllables for the melody, so it didn't scan and the effect wasn't as satisfying. And his friends laughed, plosively, the way you might laugh when a stand-up comedian insults the deaf. We all kept walking in our respective directions and you said, 'What did he say?' and I said, 'That he wanted to fuck you.' and we both laughed.

And I was thinking about dignity while I watched the fat boy being gaffer-taped to the lamp-post by his classmates, and when the girl pulled down his trousers I shouted out, 'Hey!' and they either didn't hear me or they ignored me, so I shouted, 'Hey!' again, without thinking about what I was going to say next, assuming that the presence of another human being would be enough to embarrass them into stopping. The girl looked up and shouted, 'What?' so I called out, 'Stop that!' and she shouted, 'It's okay, he likes it!' and the fat boy shouted, 'Yeah, it's okay. Thanks anyway.'

And I was thinking about dignity and about how really it's a gift you get given sometimes, like free tickets to a music festival or house-sitting for some friends in their really nice house. And you can drink protein shakes and work out a lot until you're strong enough to take dignity by force, but that's sort of like breaking and entering your friends' really nice house and sitting on their comfortable sofa, surrounded by the small things they've thought were beautiful over the years, leafing through their first edition Hemingway novels and drinking their good wine. Sooner or later they're going to get home from the ballet and say, 'What the hell are you doing here? Get out of our house!' Where their house signifies a collective sense of decency, you understand.

The Death of Us All

What had passed between us now looked like the colour-saturated
cover of a fantasy novel – and neither of us wanted to be seen
    reading it in public.
The embossed gold cage swinging low over the soft hills
as absolutely fragile as our belief in an artist –
a paper-thin glass snake in a cement labyrinth, the wiring
so complex it takes a team of five puppeteers to move it
as much as an inch. Three channels up and disrupted,
the disturbed boy sits with a 2,000 piece jigsaw puzzle
of the pyramids. He takes your hand and it feels awkward,
like a stranger palming you a betting slip.
The drama you wrote set between two wafers of an ice cream,
the drama you wrote set in a Ford Fiesta's exhaust pipe
have nothing to add to this. The only thing you can help him
with is the jigsaw puzzle. Visiting hours trip the locks.
His parents are dressed as the dummies in charity store windows.
'Your father worked three years of nightshifts to buy that
    chandelier
and I'd like you to excise all sarcastic references to it from your
    oeuvre forthwith,' says the mother.
On being liked: you can hear the wires snap, one every year.

II
More Hubris

Dolphin with a Time Machine

Novel narrated by a little hologrammatic dolphin sticker

We lived on the glittering road between the disputed
   territory
and a giant robot wedding cake. I exaggerate.
There were so many neighbouring planets, their moons
looming billiard ball size in our own sky.
We looked down at our ½ complete tax returns.
We looked up and they were watermelons.
We looked down at our ⅔ complete tax returns.
We looked up and they were hot-air balloons.
We looked down at our ¾ complete tax returns.
It was like waking up to find a face right in your face.
Our newspaper, *The Slate Blue Sky*, was perennially blank.
We all wore silver crowns which fastened under our chins.
If you died you still had a week to get your shit together.
Black and white photos of really colourful places:
our only artform. Our brains were roughly half the size
of the things we were trying to think with them.
A series of increasingly unsubtle juxtapositions
made us realise how badly we treated one another.
But what did a lifetime's erudition used to get you?
1. You married someone sexy. 2. Alcohol made either *you*
Or *me* more interesting. I forget which. Forgive us:
we were unimpressed. We sought a preliminary firmament,
relevant epaulettes and a prevalence of clover.
You gave us the equivalent of a clavinova. Hell
in a rice-paper screen that kept tearing, signed off
Yours, Ambivalent of Pensacola. Pranks followed
like ushers telling us to put out our cigarettes.
The pranks were actually beating your enemies to death
with their own walrus-faced daughters. At the ringside

I didn't know whether to grind my teeth together
until they fell apart or run yelping out of the dust-storm:
that's how cute you were. The drunk registrar found me
dying, muttered, 'If I could stop laughing I'd give you CPR.'
I usurped the duck whose beak wouldn't shut right.
Our most overpaid scenesters were cremated in the
     anteroom.
We floated out on iridescent smokescreens singing
half-baked revisionist anthems to our girlfriends –
unfortunately it was brilliant. The week was up.
In the afterlife none of us recognised one another,
as if we had chosen permanent bad dreams
but still had to make the most of it now we'd pitched camp.
We looked up and they were tax return forms.
Those of us pre-ordained to be ordained muttered
official secrets into our sleeve-mounted microphones.
I think the password is, *Ape with the trust fund, spare us.*
My cabinet: a giraffe, a unicorn, some kind of bear,
all turquoise. We got your attention on purpose
now there is nothing you can send after us.
Your microscopic robots were no match for my
microscopic will to get better. All turquoise the evening
suffocates every fraternal impulse like a factory
filled with the smoke of burned novelties.
You learned numerous stunts, but so what? So did we.
Your Attempt on my Life has Backfired topped
the charts for the 7th week running. Your soul
has been absorbed into a very thin hospital pillow
and then as a virus into a doctor's obsolete PalmPilot.
There is no time to acknowledge your concerns

and in any case you started it. Retreat to your real world.
There is nothing arbitrary about any of your sisters.
Your letter has been deliberately dropped in our breakfast:
I forgive you. (I don't really forgive you.)
Your braggadocio may yet reduce you to a baking tray.
I have eaten a galaxy compressed to the size of a grin,
I think of you as a cupcake: every bite makes me uglier;
I have walked around with all mental illnesses in my
    armpit;
tragedy was invented by my team of indolent fosters
sleeping through the day and night to bring you a more
meaningful smell which you wasted on salves;
there are senses I haven't even bothered to *try* let alone
    name;
tranches of grandeur fall out with my eyelashes.
When I submitted this as a draft it came back with
MORE HUBRIS in bold foot-high gold-embossed letters.
The Manchurians were crestfallen. Everything is cold.
The men you sent to assault me have all been folded
into their own penises and sewn up. They now hang
on the edge of town like vegetable cocoons.
Back on the Hell Screen the battle is played out
in "exquisite brush strokes" but little to no vigour.
Your General is looking at computerised breasts.
I don't want to sound like a defeatist, but *sheesh*.
I would massacre the collectors if that wasn't
exactly what they wanted. On watery Saturday nights
prophets can be recognised by their hunted expression.
Such tendentious souls have to be cooked just so,
seared lightly. It was ever thus. It all takes place

as if refracted in one of my glitter tears and will,
doubtless, be dismissed as complete scree and lightning
from the most moribund North Sea brain rig,
but it's taking place wherever the words are not
backed with silence. Do you hear it? There.

Spaceships with Guns Bigger than the Spaceships Themselves

Football is a shoot 'em up with one bullet.
Favour the animated waves, beings made of light,

the way they undulate before you kill them:
this is how we would like to encounter the other,

with kind permission. Why imaginary spaceships
look like contemporary kitchens/bathrooms,

their Dettol canons. But you, green walnut head,
put us right back in our ill-fitting safari gear.

Everything is elegant on the atomic level:
naked wizards in formation and nobody laughing.

This is a generic "biker" smashing your head
through the pinball table's glass case

because all costume is costume. Again, the "biker"
stamping an ice sheet, cracking a crème brulée.

You are thinking, 'Cat in a spaceship, cat in a spaceship.'
Now he is asking if you enjoyed it. Well?

I think he is a "sarcastic biker": his tattoos
self-portraits, b&w. This is when they steal all colour

by disappointing or shocking the whole world.
Your car resprayed metallic-No-Longer-Relevant,

evil by a moment's inattention.
May God judge you for what you did in GTA.

Your last words are recorded on a gyroscope
by some idiot who thinks gyroscopes record sound.

Partial Inheritance

If the rodent and the wizard gently sieve
the bugs and paintballs from the right to pay,
make *Asteroids* the last grand narrative,
what should we build on those foundations, eh?
The coins, piano-soft, fall from the sky,
we juggle televisions on our heads,
a dog sits on the toilet reading why
the riots happened, sleeping with the zeds
of Tsar czars, czar Tsars, Zsa Zsas and kittens
rowing backwards to the motherland.
Ignore the clown in stocks: your life depends
on whether anybody tipped the band.
May we suggest you take the bitter pill
with no sophistication but some skill.

Too Elaborately Wired

For the 2007 screenwriter strike

Simon has gone out for eight stag-dos at once
so we play boardgames: *Who Will Save us from the Squid?*
and my favourite: *Sketch Your Ego!*
Mine fills the page slowly with Biro ink;
Miranda's is a puppet too elaborately wired to move
more than a hand every month. Miranda,
I realise in the first flush of drunkenness,
is so hurtfully beautiful I start screaming:
'GAAAAAAAAAAAAAAAAAAAAAAAAAAH!'
which she takes pretty well, placing a dishcloth
over my head, reciting Psalms in plainsong.

On-screen, our favourite adventures
are still being filled-in by the writers' lunch orders.
EXT. DAY. A rainforest with muddy tracks.
A 4x4 skids to a halt pursued by a jeep.
Soldiers file out of the jeep shouting,
'PASTRAMI ON RYE! PASTRAMI ON RYE!'
Jezebel looks meaningfully at Matthias and says,
'Could you make *doubly sure* it's a soy-latte this time?
I swear I could taste dairy yesterday and, you know.'
Matthias, weeping, says, 'Waldorf in a white baguette –
and *for goodness sake* no butter – anyone who has
butter *AND* mayo in the same sandwich I wanna . . .
I don't know. I wanna squeeze their heads
and knee them in the crotch. Bleuch. Seriously.'
And the soldiers open fire, screaming,
'AND A GLUTEN-FREE POPPY-SEED MUFFIN!'

The Birds Sell Out

The raven has turned his intuition into a program.
The seagull lapses into self-parody.
Even the magpie's ego is outstripped by the hype
    surrounding him.
The thrush is remarkable only for his curious ability
to remain in the public consciousness.
The nightingale has been phoning it in for years now.
The swallow finally succumbs to sentimentality.
The warbler's lament is the lament of the jester
who suddenly wants to be taken seriously by the other
    courtiers.
The rock pipit's autohagiography is embarrassing
given that nobody you speak to has even heard of him.
I stretch. Today was a cardboard window in a calendar;
a terrified field mouse is somewhere.
Apparatchiks read their fan mail on the green.

Some Svengali You Turned Out To Be

The last permutational prose poem I will ever write

We were applauded just for being alive. The adult attempts to saw the world in half. The child obeys him.

We were applauded for our 'fallen into a toybox' look. The adult attempts to justify the harshest cruelties and egotism of his friend through a sincere examination of his own conscience. The child pushes him into a shark tank.

We were applauded for our no nonsense take on the infantilism of our generation. The adult is left blank for your own message. The child is SORRY YOU'RE LEAVING.

We were applauded for our delicious stuffing mix. The adult cannot remember for the life of him why he went downstairs and has gone upstairs to jog his memory – or was he downstairs in the first place and must go back there to jog his memory about why he is now upstairs? The child has remained stationary throughout and is wearing your spectacles.

We were applauded for not taking you too seriously when you said our whole practice was built on bogus foundations. The adult just said his first sincere thing today at twenty minutes past three. The child will be right with you after he finishes reading comment number 16 under an Amazon review of a novel he hasn't read, but suspects has been poorly served by its amateur critics; 'To what tributary,' he mutters, 'to what run-off pool have I channelled my thoughts?'

We were applauded for our bogus foundations. The adult snaps a chocolate bar in half and admires an edifice. The child kicks over a city.

We were applauded for self-loathing and self-publishing. The adult's favourite question is 'Any thoughts?' The child's raised eyebrow is more than sufficient.

We were applauded for diminishing returns and doing the washing up. The adult takes work where it can find it. The child carries all your furniture downstairs, piece by piece.

We were applauded for the inherent limitations of our craft. The adult was killed in an explosion. The child is skilled at exposition.

We were applauded for endless repetition. The adult attempts to compose herself, the child outruns its own programme.

Antidote to Curses #1-17

BEING A REINSTIGATION OF FREEWILL FOLLOWING ITS SUSPENSION

Paint an eye on the underside of your pillow.
Late November, quit your job without explanation.
Sit in an orange chair. Take out a guitar.
When someone looks you directly in the eye
play a single, ringing minor chord.
Press guitar to your face. Inhale the pencil smell.
Stand up, letting guitar fall to the floor.
Walk very slowly towards the window.
When close enough, kiss your reflection.
Next morning I will be at a market stall,
looking at cheap batteries. 'Do you really think
they work as well as, you know, the *label* ones?'
I'll ask you. In our developing friendship
I will be argumentative with your partner,
more than is appropriate or reasonable
and about subjects which to him/her are sensitive.
And though we have only just met you will feel divided.
Ultimately you will want rid of me, but I will turn up
7am and crying when you are trying to get ready for work
and because it is very important to you
that other people see you as a nice person
you will comfort me and I will say thank you
thank you for being my friend when nobody else will.
Let's go to a Chinese restaurant. You will have chicken satay.
Your partner cannot believe you're still seeing me.
He/she calls me, 'The Asshole' 'You're going to see
a film with The Asshole? That's great.
have a good time. Send The Asshole my best.'
Next day we're going to walk around the town centre
until someone asks you if you want a free stress test.

Hold onto their lapels.[1] Hold fast. Unleash everything.
Scream. Let go of it all. Your hurt feelings, your acts of cruelty,
that half-sense you cannot name. Do you feel –
we are in Starbucks now, drinking lattes the size of poster-
    tubes –
do you feel the curse has lifted? Do you?
I'm glad I was able to do this one small thing for you
after you've been there for me, come through time and again,
unwaveringly; one day I'll read this at your funeral.

---

[1] If they do not have lapels, hold onto their hair. If they do not have hair,
hold onto their lapels. It is very rare that they will have neither.

Wolf Shibboleth

Before Annabelle leaves she likens us to newsreaders when the lights dim a semi-tone and the credits roll.

'You lean over to make a joke so I can say something which looks natural,' she says. 'And when it doesn't work, you throw your clipboard at me.'

'You think too much, Annabelle,' I tell her.

I am painting a little pewter figurine of the wolf. I am painting his lips mauve.

'Besides, I'm tired,' she says, softly closing the lime-green front door we've never stripped. Its click is like a cold chocolate bar snapping.

The wolf arrives less than fifteen minutes later. He quickly goes in and out of every room in the house.

'*Again?*' he says. 'Oh, for the love of God.'

'She thinks too much,' I tell him.

'Evidently,' says the wolf. 'As for me, I have retrained as a phonologist and independent scholar. My next book is to be called *The Escapology of Eschatology*. Or *The Eschatology of Escapology*. I've not decided yet. There are interviews for a chair at your local university, so if you don't mind.'

The wolf sets his hat box on top of his steamer trunk and slaps it like a horse.

II

'In my research so far I have learned that there are two types of "U",' says the wolf, '"U" and "non-U". It was originally invented as an after-dinner card game, but people took offence at it something awful. The War, I suppose.'

'What on earth are you talking about?' I fold my copy of *How to Solve Cryptic Crosswords* over my cryptic crossword. The wolf pours the coffee and says something inaudible.

'Pardon?' I say.

'Oh, *very* clever,' says the wolf. '"Pardon", eh? Trying to pass as a chimney sweep, I suppose. The point is, I have worked out,' he rearranges a bunch of papers and adjusts his spectacles, 'why you make people so uncomfortable. It is your accent.'

'My accent is quite similar to yours,' I tell him.

'But mine doesn't count,' says the wolf. 'I have the necessary poise and elegance to pull it off. You're an Ephraimite, I'm a Gileadite.'

'What does that have to do with anything?'

'When the world ends, quite a lot, actually,' says the wolf. 'I have written a list poem to illustrate my point. It's not very good – it's not finished, really. I hate it. Do I *have* to read it to you?'

'I'm sure it's all right,' I pat him on the paw.

'I'm joking,' says the wolf, 'It's brilliant as usual.'

III

The wolf assumes his "poetry reading" stance.

You have the voice of the oppressor,
The voice of the second-home owner,
The voice of the privately educated, the well-fed,
The voice of the diplomat, ambassador, arms dealer,
The voice of the pedant, the asset-stripper,
The voice of the slave-driver, the colonial, the
    consulate,
The voice of false modesty,
The voice of *my client will take that as advised*,
The voice of *this is unacceptable*,
The voice of inheritance, capital, private income,
The voice of the news circa 1960,
The voice of the eleven course after-dinner speaker,
The voice of the fox hunter, the sherry drinker,
The voice that had everything handed to it on a plate,
A really nice plate,
A voice that did not work its way up from nothing,
A voice which did not start this company with £1 and a
    dream,
A voice the sole purpose of oppositional art is to make
    splutter, 'Wh- What? This isn't *art!*'
A voice your contemporaries worked out it might
    be a good idea to drop about three months into
    secondary school.

'What do you think?' he says, twiddling his tail.

'It's a bit listy,' I say.

'*You're* a bit listy,' says the wolf. 'Anyway, it doesn't matter what you think as I have already published it.'

IV

The wolf and I clean the living room with dusters and wood polish. A robin lands on the windowsill. It looks through the glass with its head cocked to one side, as if it were about to say, *'Really?'* Its chest inflates and deflates like a little balloon about to pop.

'Anyone can tell you are posh because you have a cheap television,' says the wolf, spraying the big dark-grey television with wood polish. 'You got it from a charity shop for £20 and when it breaks you will get another one, also for £20. That is very "U". The average price of a "non-U" television is £1,799.99 It is so flat and thin you can't even *see* it sideways-on and it is also very shiny. The difference is this: The "U" don't want people to think that they care about television.'

'That's as maybe,' I tell him, 'but I got my sofa on credit. I'll still be paying for it in three years.'

'And yet you call it a *sofa*,' says the wolf.

'World of Sofas calls it a sofa,' I protest.

'Next it'll be "looking glass" and "chimney piece",' says the wolf. 'Next you'll be calling the

Jack of Clubs the *Knave of Collywobbles*. You might as well wear a monocle.'

'These are all pretty out-dated examples,' I tell him.

'Class was invented by the Finnish Journal of Linguistics in 1952,' says the wolf. 'So of *course* they're outdated. How about this room? Do you call it the lounge or the drawing room?'

'The living room.'

'You fucking coward,' says the wolf.

V

'I'll talk you through it,' says the wolf. 'A history
lesson. This will help me practice for my
"Chair" interview in a couple of months' time.'

It is twilight and we are sitting in the living
room, which smells like a brand new coffin.
We are eating spaghetti carbonara. The wolf
has opened a bottle of room-temperature
champagne explaining that it is very "non-U" to
care about cold drinks.

Whenever my eyes rest on a photograph
of Annabelle it's like seeing a picture of a
Hollywood starlet from another era. That's how
much I miss her.

'At one stage it was desirable to imitate the
language of your betters,' says the wolf. 'So
we attached great importance to whether
somebody said "Pardon?" or "What?" when
they didn't hear you. The "U" said "What?"
because they were self-assured enough to be
obnoxious. The "non-U" said "Pardon" because
they mistakenly believed it was good manners.
But really they wanted to say "What?" as much
as their betters, only they couldn't because Ma
would cuff them with a rolling-pin. The betters

called a rolling-pin a "Poor Man's Barge Pole", which they thought frightfully amusing.'

'Where are you getting this from?'

'But now it's about not wanting to appear privileged,' the wolf continues. 'Everybody wants everybody else to think that they had to work harder than they really did for the things they have. Some "U"s even have their ears removed so as to not appear "U", hence the phrase: "He's as much sense as an earless-U." There is also the North/South divide.'

'How does that relate?'

'You wouldn't understand,' says the wolf.

VI

'At a time of great deprivation, a voice like yours is more than a social embarrassment; it is a liability,' says the wolf. 'Therefore it is not so much about saving face as it is about survival. What would you call this steamed pudding? Dessert, I suppose?' The wolf pours custard out of the mixing jug.

'It *is* a pudding,' I say, 'but we're having it for dessert.'

'And the overall meal?'

'Supper.'

'This is a complete disaster,' spits the wolf. 'People hear your voice and they want to smash their pint glass and cut out your tongue.'

'I'm not sure it's ever going to come to that,' I say.

'You wait,' says the wolf. 'You sound like the politicians explaining that we all have to make sacrifices. Say it. Go on. Say it.'

'We all have to make sacrifices,' I say.

The wolf opens a fourth bottle of passable Rioja.
The cork sounds like a stupid person being
mildly surprised.

'The point is: nobody likes sacrifices,' says the
wolf. 'Especially human or livestock sacrifices,
and furthermore nobody likes politicians – I
have observed this on television. Therefore you
can be doubly certain that nobody likes *you*,
so it seems to me that you have two choices:
downplay or exaggerate your personality.'

'Either that or not worry so much about what
other people –'

'I'm sorry,' the wolf interrupts, 'I couldn't hear
you through all of the silver spoons slapping
out of your mouth.'

VII

We have slept through breakfast so I prepare a
nauseating lunch of bloody marys and tomato
soup. The combination of ice-cold and piping
hot tomato is a unique and ghastly punishment
for I know not what.

'The thing is,' says the wolf, 'we're all the
same, really. The "U" is as perfectly miserable
drinking a post-opera gin and tonic in his
private blimp as the "non-U" is with his
pint of bitter in the public house after a
long day's meat packing. My solution is the
Democratisation of Hats.'

The wolf produces a silly looking hat. It is red
and has several strings attached to miniature
games.

'With everyone wearing the same cheerful hat,
there'll be no easy way to differentiate and
everyone can distract themselves from the
human condition with the attached novelties.
Also, the hat contains a tiny phial of time-
release poison, so that everybody dies of the
same disease at exactly the same time.'

'It's brilliant,' I tell him, stirring half a can of
milk into the Campbell's tomato soup.

'Sarcasm,' says the wolf, sadly. 'It's all very well for someone like you to make light of it –'

'Listen,' I tell him, 'In 21st century Britain there are two classes and one of them is homeowners. The rest of us are going to have to ask our landlords' permission to hang up a painting or have children or to host our own wakes. And the landlords will be all like, "Oh, no, I don't really want a *corpse* in my nice clean house, even if it's only for an afternoon. I'm sure you understand."'

'I'd advise you not to get ideas above your station,' growls the wolf. 'Everyone's going to be dead of poison in forty-four years anyway.'

VIII

The wolf is offered and accepts the Chair of
Phonology, using me as a case study.

'Your genius is in combining the worst habits
of the "U" and the "non-U",' says the wolf.
'You drink too much, you're *boring*, you
have a chip *and* an inverted chip on your
shoulder and you harp on and on about both
of them, your vocabulary is a little "try-hard",
your enunciation a mixture of out-dated
and American sitcom teenager, you're
simultaneously contemptuous and universally
sycophantic, you're snobbish about books, films
and music, but you're dismissive of interior
design and architecture, you eat at McDonalds
one day and a Michelin starred restaurant
the next, you're capable of being crass and
oversensitive in the same sentence, you're
useless with money, you're in massive debt
and yet you pay into a savings account, you're
desperate for people to like you, even though
you secretly hate *everyone*. We ran metrics on
all of your data and it turns out that you're
exactly middle class. The absolute median. To
five decimal places. I mean, the department
loved it. You're basically a celebrity.'

'I'm very happy for you,' I tell him. 'Crack open the warm champagne.'

'For a mere £9,000 a year, children will learn of the intricacies of the class system from one of the foremost experts in the field.' says the wolf. 'A new dawn. I start in September with a six month sabbatical.'

Leather-Bound Road

Should anybody ask me how we met I'll read them
Ansel Adams on photography and say it's in
the way the artist brings out of the landscape
what the frame brings out of the painting.
Which is to say you bring out the best in me,
but not the way the Maillard reaction
brings out the best in food through the combination
of amino acids, reducing sugars and heat.
It's more the way the right wine brings out the right light
and the scene reflected in your eye places me
front and centre, peering in, trying to describe the colour.
It's what the singer does between the words
that makes the words *the words* and not just words.
The way the crows that currant-stud the risen green
don't startle as I cycle through and crunch the gears.
Distracted weavers weave their hair into the tapestry,
a knight which leapt six hours ago makes sense now.
The way the symphony opens up only when you know
what's coming next, your place in it and why (or not).
The way the past's not even past and looking back
I overlooked the beauty of the worst of it.
The exam flunked, the form misfiled, the blown bulb
and the curtain drawn which caused the bar's inviting glow.
This way that led with more coincidence and happenstance
than a minor Victorian novel and yet with the absolute
conviction of its binding, and with gratitude, to you.

III

No More Kings

Venerable Old Writer

Showtune #5 From The Necropolis Boat

When I'm a venerable old writer
with the misfortune to outlive you
I'll marry someone much younger
and passably attractive
with an undiagnosed condition
and I'll bequeath my estate to her
and leave nothing to our children
when I die three years later.

How my biographer will hate her
as she sequesters correspondence,
loses early drafts and memos,
drops my diaries in the fire
and tries to turn us all against him,
(which will work: he's irritating).
Sue for unfair dismissal – see if I care
when I'm a venerable old writer.

I'll take long nature walks without you
thinking about my detractors
I'll miss you like a fan misses their fictional world
once the film ends, once the book ends.
And while our friends' concern is touching
I won't return their calls or wash up
the baking trays of their lasagnes
because my grief will be like white noise.

My brain will nurture its resentments:
an old car that fills with cobwebs –
I'll say I never really liked them
I'll say our marriage was a sham.
That sound's our daughter hammering the door in.
What have you done? Did you learn nothing
from all eleven of your novels?
The endings never were your strong point.

Haunted Zoetrope

Decommissioned ekphrastic poem on
Jeff Koons's 'Popeye' sequence

The fact is all of us are going to live
roughly the same amount of time
to the nearest fifty years.
The planet as Etch-a-Sketch.
No, seriously, come back.

    Concept 1:
    – Lines of dialogue from Popeye cartoon/strip, e.g.
      (Wikipedia records it as, "A-gah-gah-gah-gah-gah-
      gah!"
    Whereas I hear, "Ug-ug-ug-ug-ug-ug-ug-ug!")
    – Sentences from copy of pornographic magazine/novel
    – Lines of safety instructions for children's' inflatable.
    The above rendered as beautifully crafted sonnet
      (to mirror photorealistic oil on canvas –
      sense of vertigo when you look close up).
    But you have a team of sixty working on 10cm^2 patches,

'All of this is just computerised hair,' she said.
'Something you want to give yourself to, or not.'

One day we stand at the same dock, our expressions of
defiance suddenly recontextualised as loss, what was
strength, incomprehension.

    'Actually I think there are few more repressed than the
      S&M crowd,
    Their spooky music, their insisting that the slightest thing
      be named, every spark, every impulse:

[67]

'FRESCO ENTITLED ADAM NAMES THE PERVERSIONS.

'Well, most of us are pretty comfortable with the whole
    sex/power thing, guys.
When we come we think of illuminated manuscripts and
    being liked.'

I've built a booth where a cartoon priest gives you penance.
I was going through my phase of calling everything an act of
    violence:
Making a paperweight, educating a child, the postal system.

I am somewhere between the famous model in the hair dye
advert and the not-famous model on the hair dye packaging.

    Backing vocal: 'Where's our cheque?'

My photo albums ('PRECIOUS MEMORIES' – change this) are
all magazine clippings and people from packaging. I speak of
them as images of me.

This one is me eating a hot-dog, looking at a photo of a woman
in a bikini eating a hotdog. Except I'm not pictured: my
presence is manifested by this four year old mustard stain.

The cartoon priest delivers your penance as a show tune
which is, in a way, its own punishment.

Long-running daily soap opera shot by Tarkovsky.
DJ, happily, 'We're TIRED, TIRED, TIRED!'

And under hobbies and interests you've put:
Hoping women's' skirts get blown up by the breeze.
And there's . . . there's nothing else on the page.
Is that really your *only* interest?

"Let's not judge the asshole: he's been through a lot."

And are you not ashamed of that?
Um . . . A little. I guess.

Cut in stone: I'M SO SORRY FOR RUINING ALL OF YOUR
LIVES. Bind-weed growing over the letters.

World made of hair.

Everyone was terrified when we heard the tiny brightly
coloured men were on their way, but when they arrived they
only said, 'We forgive you.'

'We forgive you, we forgive you, we forgive you.'

The Lovely Crime Scene

I want the world to be transfigured
like a crime scene. The way every scrap
suddenly matters: scalp flakes,
binned notes, dried fluids, apple core.
The model on the hair dye packaging:
a tell-tale blood splotch on his cardboard cheek.
I want it to be early spring so that
the cello's topknot perfect-rhymes
the curl of the unripe fern and your
thin fingers pick the branches bare before
keystone forensic scientists arrive,
careening in their looming car soundtracked
by a piano falling down the stairs.
Their canes match black, gold-filtered cigarettes.
If I am murdered, keep it from the press:
don't let my eulogy be buried under
stamp-sized puerile General Interest squibs.
Rather let me lie dying long enough
to leave a patch of yellowed, thickened grass
so passing children might assume the park
had borne a tent or trampoline; the bounce
as temporary as joy. As necessary.

[Jeremiah]

[Man in his 30s, professional. Shirt and jacket, tie.]

Let's say I already know this is going to fail. This'll be easier if I try to give you an analogy. A parable. Okay. Let's say I'm running a cattery. No, let's say I'm trying to *steal business* from an existing cattery by touting my own domestic cattery outside the official cattery gates. "A home from home for your precious cat!" is my catch-phrase. Unfortunately I underestimated the public's disenchantment with the official cattery. One in two, two in three; they come to me instead. I've taken six car loads back to my house already. I'm starting to regret it. I'm allergic to cat fur. I've been inundated with cats. Scores of them. I can't afford all the food. I don't remember whose cat was whose. Some of the cats are dead. The constant yowling and meowing . . . No, actually, that isn't what I'm trying to say at all . . .

Say I'm preparing a meal. Do we have any amateur chefs here tonight? No, start again. Say I'm site manager on a building project. We're building a utopian housing solution. An anti-tower block. Anti- everything the tower block has come to represent. It's only three stories high. It covers a square mile. There are parks and ponds within its walls; they're covered and heated, because, you know, the weather in this country. Our message to the people who're

[71]

gonna live there: We love you. You're worth all of this land.

But here's the thing: my boys, my team, they don't do any work. The foundations are down, the scaffolding's up, but my team have started, what do the Americans call it? "Goofing off". That's right. They're goofing off. Nothing is getting built. Nothing. I expect a little horseplay. I expect euphemisms coarser and more offensive than the terms they substitute. That means you simultaneously say the thing you were going to say, you say it in a more grotesque manner while paying sarcastic lip-service to the oversensitivity of your audience. I expect euphemisms coarser and more offensive than the terms they substitute. And I expect that to map onto their behaviour more generally. Did you know euphemism used to mean 'keeping a holy silence'? To speak well by not speaking. I don't expect a holy silence.

But this has got nasty. They have a 25 gallon plastic waterbutt – they've sawed it in half. It contains ice and cans of lager. They call it "Matilda". I don't know why. They've made hammocks out of the chrome struts and ropes.

They climb to the top of the scaffolding and drop breeze-blocks on each other's heads: nobody's died yet, but we've had some bad concussions. They laugh at each other's concussions. They say, 'Duhhh! Look at Steve! Buhhhh! He's *drooling!*' They have league tables of successful concussions.

They chase one another with drills. They play chicken with the forklifts. I am trying to account for the writing-off or serious damage to three forklifts.

They play Russian roulette with pornography on their smartphones. Six of them stand in a circle and . . . No, actually it's too unpleasant. 'Never tell someone something you wouldn't tell me.' That's what my mum used to tell me.

Also, there are three rival contractors working on the same building and I'm supposed to be overseeing all of them, although there's been a mistake and they all think they have responsibility for the same process.

But my company have had this idea. There are big speakers arranged all up and down the scaffolding and I have a contact mic attached to my tie. Whatever I say, they have to listen, they have no choice. Whenever I try to speak into the mic: squawks of feedback. It's loud. Feels like it physically touches your brain. That's all I can do – cause them to momentarily stop whatever they're doing and writhe in agony for a few seconds.

This has made me unpopular.

And anyway, it's being built on a flood plane, the utopian housing solution. And being a low-riser, it's at high risk. And anyway, my father, who owns the construction firms' umbrella company, is about to pull the plug on the project. Umbrellas, plugs. What is it with me and water?

And anyway, my grandfather, who used to run the country, is about to start a civil war. So basically my utopian housing solution is going to be knee deep in septic water. And there will be bodies floating in it. That's if it ever reaches completion. Which it won't. I tell them I wish I'd never been born. It comes out as ear-piercing feedback.

[Irritated.] No, start again. Say I'm preparing a meal.

[Lights down. Up again.]

Let's say you're on a sinking car ferry. You're stuck in your car – the doors are jammed and the boat's going under. They've only just given up trying to cut you out, they've thrown up their hands. Only one of them could make eye-contact with you. He grimaced. Mouthed, 'I'm sorry.' They've staggered away. Smell of oil, petrol, salt. The car rolls into the ferry's back wall. A half finished roll of extra-strong mints strikes you on the forehead. Your daughter's star-shaped plastic sunglasses strike you on the forehead. Your mobile starts ringing, it's me, and I say, 'Bad news ...'

[Lights down. Up again.]

Let's say I take my trousers off. I'm not going to take my trousers off. Let's say that I do, though. I take them off and I walk through the office I work in and nobody says anything. I leave the office by the revolving doors. I wait for the person coming in to push the door. I let them do the work. I take the trousers and I go to an alleyway, a dirty alleyway at the side of the office, and I stuff the trousers into the gutter. Nobody sees me do it. The next week I go back and I retrieve the trousers. They're ruined. I try to . . . No, they're good for nothing.

Some people see me doing this. I tell them it's a symbolic act. They're just like *[Rolls eyes.]* 'Yeah, okay.'

'If you are well brought up,' I tell them, 'you don't roll your eyes at anyone. You don't question why somebody does something. If you see someone with no trousers talking about symbolic acts, you put your arm around them. You offer them your trousers. Your first thought is always, how can I help this poor, poor man? That's what I mean by well brought up,' I tell them.

[Lights down. Up again.]

Let's say I tell you a story about our last business conference. Hey, come back! It's a good story. I set the scene: We're in a modern room panelled-up to look like a traditional pub. There's a fake open fire. Me, Richard and several of my senior colleagues are sitting on leather sofas around a table by the fake open fire. I'm drinking this whisky called Mortloch, which I guess means *the lake of death*. Death *is* like a lake, I tell him. Do you not just want to try it? I say. It's amazing! It's the best whisky ever! It tastes like train sets and old books! We are at a business conference and I know full well that Richard is a recovering alcoholic. His smile of forbearance is *just* starting to slip. Just one little sip! I tell him. Our colleagues stare at me in horror. Samantha mutters that I'm just trying to get attention, and whether she's right or not, it appears to have worked. I have your attention. You're in there too. You haven't worked for the company long. You're pretty. I haven't noticed it. Others have. I take you aside. I tell you that you have to remember my purposes in telling you this story may be quite different to the reasons I had for doing it in the first place. *[Pause.]* Let's say I'm preparing a meal, but ... No.

[Lights down. Up again.]

Let's say I've just started laughing out loud in the middle of your friend's funeral. Loud, fake laughter. And what offends you is not the laughter *per se*, but its disingenuousness. *[Pause.]* Are not all my words fire and a hammer that shatters rock?

[Lights down. Up again.]

Let's say I'm at a party and I'm talking to you. You can't work out if I'm nice or slightly creepy. I tell you that the English have a figure of speech. The English have a lot of figures of speech, I tell you. But this is one of them. We say, It's second nature to him now. Maybe rock-climbing, water skiing. It's become second nature to him. But that's a misappropriation, I tell you. You're eating a pretzel. That's not the point. We had a first nature, I tell you. *We had a first nature* is the point. You take another pretzel. You are deciding that I am creepy. I don't want to sound preachy or anything, I tell you.

[Lights down. Up again.]

The other prophets were insane; that was the feeling among the prophets. Which is to say each prophet thought as much about his fellow prophets who bit their own fingers when they ate, if they ate at all, and whose struggles, which were real enough, seemed at best a delusion, at worst affectation.

[Lights fade to spot. Points at member of audience.]

You were on your way to the supermarket to buy coriander for the soup you were making. You were thinking about picking the kids up after school. In the morning you had argued with your significant other and you still felt kind of bruised from that. We were a pretty off-putting bunch, all told.

[Lights down. Up again.]

Let's say I've invited you to a Pop Art exhibition in a warzone. I'm giving a paper. You don't want to offend me, so you agree to come along. I'm on 8th. First I drop a clay pot on the stage and it smashes. Then I insult the art exhibited around me. I say it's *comfortable*. I say complacency is the last thing to which contemporary art should aspire. I say it's dull. I say the artists clearly don't know the first thing about art. I say the problem is we have started to derive sexual pleasure from one another's suffering. That this was the inevitable end-result of our cruelty, our gluttony, our profligacy, and that this is the only real problem, that we derive sexual pleasure from one another's suffering. That any art which fails to address this central question of our time is worse than useless. Outside: airstrikes.

[*Lights down. Up again.*]

Let's say I tell you about my dad's friend who was in a car accident. It was winter, icy, a cloud had settled low on the city. He piled into a tree. He lost blood. He almost died. He talks about it as if it were the best thing that ever happened to him. He had this vision that everything around him burst into flower. He cries when he tells you. He can't tell you the story without breaking down. The bare branches, the scrubby liminal spaces. Let's say I'm explaining that to you through the squawks of feedback coming from the scaffold-mounted speakers. You have a handful of dry cement. A lost expression.